SNOOPY STARS

— AS —

THE GREAT PRETENDER

Charles M. Schulz

RR

RAVETTE BOOKS

First published by
Ravette Books Limited 1988
Revised 1989

Printed and bound in Great Britain
for Ravette Books Limited,
3 Glenside Estate, Star Road, Partridge Green,
Horsham, West Sussex RH13 8RA
by Cox & Wyman Ltd, Reading

ISBN 1 85304 067 3

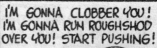

PEANUTS

THIS IS SATURDAY.. REAL VULTURES DON'T PERCH IN TREES ON SATURDAY

I DIDN'T KNOW THAT..

7-26

PEANUTS

HERE'S THE WORLD FAMOUS GROCERY CLERK TAKING UP HIS POSITION BY THE CHECK-OUT COUNTER..

TWO BREAD..THIRTY-NINE TWICE.. PEACHES...TWENTY-SEVEN... COOKIES..FORTY-NINE..PEANUT BUTTER.

HEY, FRED, HOW MUCH ON THE PEANUT BUTTER TODAY?

8-28

ACTUALLY, I KNEW THE PRICE... I JUST LIKE TO YELL AT OL' FRED..

SCHULZ

27

SORRY, KID...
THAT'S THE
WAY IT GOES!

THERE'S A VULTURE SITTING ON YOUR SNOWMAN...

ANY VULTURE CAUGHT SITTING ON MY SNOWMAN GETS CLOBBERED!

RATS!

PEANUTS HERE'S JOE COOL HANGING AROUND THE BEACH DRINKING ROOT BEER AND EYEING CHICKS

HERE'S JOE COOL IMPRESSING THE CHICKS BY CRUSHING THE EMPTY CAN WITH ONE HAND...

8-12

STUPID CAN!

SCHULZ

PEANUTS

HERE'S JOE COOL LOOKING OVER A FEW OF THE LANGUAGE COURSES FOR THIS TERM

9-22

I'M VERY HUNG-UP ON LANGUAGES... MAYBE I'LL STUDY HEBREW AND KOREAN AND SERBIAN...

HI, JOE... I SEE YOU'RE DOWN FOR BONEHEAD ENGLISH AGAIN...

❊ SIGH ❊

NO ONE EVER INVITES JOE COOL HOME FOR THANKSGIVING...

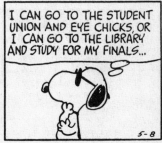

PEANUTS

YO HO HO AND A BOTTLE OF RUM!

8-14

HERE'S THE FIERCE PIRATE STANDING ON THE DECK OF HIS SHIP...

HIS FAITHFUL PARROT FLIES TOWARD HIM TO PERCH ON HIS SHOULDER...

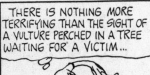

© 1988 United Feature Syndicate, Inc.   1-18

YOU KNOW WHAT'S A BAD SIGN?

WHEN YOU MEET YOUR DOCTOR IN THE HALLWAY OF THE HOSPITAL, AND HE DOESN'T RECOGNIZE YOU..

IF YOU WERE A REAL OWL, YOU KNOW WHAT YOU'D DO?

YOU'D SWOOP OUT OF YOUR TREE, AND CATCH A MOUSE

THAT'S WHAT YOU'D DO IF YOU WERE A REAL OWL

THAT'S WHAT I'D DO IF I WERE OUT OF MY MIND!

© 1977 United Feature Syndicate, Inc.

HERE'S THE WORLD FAMOUS SURVEYOR PREPARING A LAND DESCRIPTION...

"RICHARD ROE...
N 81° 02' W 184.32 ft.
S 61° 47' W 187.15 ft."

"JOHN DOE...HMM....
N 19° 45' W 285.62 ft."

6-20   © 1979 United Feature Syndicate, Inc.

EXCUSE ME..I THINK YOU'RE STANDING ON MAIN STREET

HERE'S THE REPORT ON YOUR PROPERTY..ACCORDING TO THE SURVEYOR, YOU'RE BOTH WRONG...

N91° W161

HE SAYS YOUR GARDEN BELONGS TO JOHN DOE, AND THE FARMER'S LAND BELONGS TO RICHARD ROE

WHERE IS THAT SURVEYOR? I'LL BREAK HIS BONES!

NOBODY HERE BUT US SCARECROWS

HERE'S THE FIERCE RATTLESNAKE CRAWLING ALONG THE GROUND...

© 1980 United Feature Syndicate, Inc.

HE'LL BE PETRIFIED BECAUSE HE KNOWS THERE IS NO DEFENSE AGAINST A RATTLESNAKE..

HIS VICTIM WILL BE PETRIFIED WITH FEAR

EXCEPT FOR STUFFING A BLANKET IN HIS MOUTH!

3-28

SCHULZ

IN THE TWENTY-FIRST CHAPTER OF CHRONICLES IT TELLS OF KING DAVID'S SIN IN ORDERING A CENSUS

4-4

AS A PUNISHMENT, SEVENTY THOUSAND MEN DIED IN A PLAGUE...

A PLAGUE?

YOU GO AHEAD, THOUGH... TAKE YOUR CENSUS... WE PROBABLY WON'T HAVE ANOTHER PLAGUE

MY HEAD FEELS WARM... I THINK I HAVE A SORE THROAT...

SCHULZ

© 1980 United Feature Syndicate, Inc.

WHEN YOU GO SOME PLACE NICE, YOU SHOULD ALWAYS SHINE YOUR FEET!

TRY TO KEEP THE SHIP STEADY, MEN..I'M GOING TO MY CABIN TO REST!

OKAY, HIRED HAND...
HERE'S WHAT I WANT
YOU TO DO...

I NEED THIS WHOLE
YARD SPADED SO I
CAN PLANT MY GARDEN..

ARE YOU SURE YOU'VE
DONE THIS KIND OF
WORK BEFORE?

© 1982 United Feature Syndicate, Inc.

I ALWAYS WONDERED WHAT HAPPENED TO OLD WORN-OUT HIRED HANDS

THE PHONE'S RINGING.. I'LL BE OUT IN A MINUTE TO SHOW YOU WHAT TO DO...

I'M SORRY, I CAN'T TALK TO YOU NOW... MY HIRED HAND AND I ARE PLANTING MY GARDEN...

3-8

HERE, HIRED HAND.. TAKE THESE PACKAGES OF SEEDS OUT TO THE GARDEN...

© 1982 United Feature Syndicate, Inc.

HERE'S THE WORLD FAMOUS SURGEON ON HIS WAY TO THE OPERATING ROOM...

DOCTOR, IT SAYS HERE THAT AFTER SURGERY, FIFTY PERCENT OF YOUR PATIENTS FEEL PRETTY GOOD FOR HALF AN HOUR

DO THOSE STATISTICS BOTHER YOU?

NO, I'M VERY EASY GOING

7-12

YOU SEE, MY DAD'S NAME IS JOE PUDDING SO IT WAS ONLY NATURAL THAT I'D BE CALLED TAPIOCA PUDDING..

MY DAD'S IN LICENSING, YOU KNOW

I KNOW

WITH MY NAME AND FACE ON EVERY GREETING CARD AND CEREAL BOX IN THE COUNTRY, MY DAD SAYS WE'LL MAKE A MILLION..

9-9

YOU DON'T KNOW ANYTHING ABOUT INVESTMENTS, DO YOU?

MY AGENT JUST GOT ME A PERSONAL APPEARANCE AT THE OPENING CEREMONIES OF THE OLYMPIC GAMES IN LOS ANGELES!

THE OLYMPIC GAMES WERE TWO YEARS AGO

WHERE'S THAT AGENT? I'LL POUND HIM!!

9-17

© 1986 United Feature Syndicate, Inc.

WE'D BETTER SAY GOODBYE, SWEETIE.. I LEAVE FOR FRANCE AT MIDNIGHT....

AS A WORLD FAMOUS SURGEON, DO OTHER DOCTORS OFTEN ASK FOR YOUR ADVICE?

© 1987 United Feature Syndicate, Inc.

2-19

OH, YES.. ALL THE TIME...

JUST THE OTHER DAY DR. WICK ASKED FOR MY ADVICE...

I SAID, "WELL, IT'S ABOUT A HUNDRED AND THIRTY YARDS..YOU'D BETTER HIT THE EIGHT IRON"

SURGEONS LIKE YOURSELF MUST BE UNDER A LOT OF STRESS...

WHAT DO YOU THINK ABOUT AS YOU ENTER THE OPERATING ROOM?

ARE THERE ANY THOUGHTS THAT RUN THROUGH YOUR MIND JUST BEFORE YOU BEGIN THE SURGERY?

"FEED A COLD AND STARVE A FEVER"

Other Snoopy titles published by Ravette Books

Snoopy Stars in this series

No. 1	Snoopy Stars as The Flying Ace	£1.95
No. 2	Snoopy Stars as The Matchmaker	£1.95
No. 3	Snoopy Stars as The Terror of the Ice	£1.95
No. 4	Snoopy Stars as The Legal Beagle	£1.95
No. 5	Snoopy Stars as The Fearless Leader	£1.95
No. 6	Snoopy Stars as Man's Best Friend	£1.95
No. 7	Snoopy Stars as The Sportsman	£1.95
No. 8	Snoopy Stars as The Scourge of The Fairways	£1.95
No. 9	Snoopy Stars as The Branch Manager	£1.95
No. 10	Snoopy Stars as The World Famous Literary Ace	£1.95
No. 12	Snoopy Stars as The Dog-Dish Gourmet	£1.95
No. 13	Snoopy Stars as The Fitness Freak	£1.95
No. 14	Snoopy Stars in The Pursuit of Pleasure	£1.95
No. 15	Snoopy Stars as The Weatherman	£1.95

Colour landscapes

First Serve	£2.95
Be Prepared	£2.95
Stay Cool	£2.95
Shall We Dance?	£2.95
Let's Go	£2.95
Come Fly With Me	£2.95
Are Magic	£2.95
Hit The Headlines	£2.95

Black and white landscapes

It's a Dog's Life	£2.50
Roundup	£2.50
Freewheelin'	£2.50
Joe Cool	£2.50
Chariots For Hire	£2.50
Dogs Don't Eat Dessert	£2.50
You're on the Wrong Foot Again, Charlie Brown	£2.50
By Supper Possessed	£2.95

Weekenders

No. 1 Weekender	£4.95

All these books are available at your local bookshop or news-agent, or can be ordered direct from the publisher. Just tick the titles you require and fill in the form below. Prices and availability subject to change without notice.

Ravette Books Limited, 3 Glenside Estate, Star Road, Partridge Green, Horsham, West Sussex RH13 8RA

Please send a cheque or postal order, and allow the following for postage and packing. UK: Snoopy Stars – 45p for one book, 20p for a second book and 15p for each additional book. Other titles – 50p for one book and 30p for each additional book.

Name ....

Address ....

....